M000312647

JAPAN

IMAGINE & DISCOVER

HERRON

Contents

Introduction

There's something irresistible about Japan. Its futuristic technology, jaunty sushi trains, out-there fashion statements, edgy anime, and perky J-pop have been exported across the globe, bringing the average Westerner much closer to this erstwhile insular nation than at any other point in its history.

The more we know, the more we want to go. Perhaps not only for the glare of neon signs, the reach of sky towers, or to buy the latest gadget. No, this beguiling nation lures the visitor dreaming of gardens resplendent in cherry blossoms, of ancient temples rising from the sea or nestling in the ragged slopes of a mountain, or the sight of geisha walking down cobblestoned streets past centuries-old wooden houses. These images take hold in the imagination and linger there until seen in the flesh.

Adventurous types are sure to be seduced by a land that's so generously endowed with gifts by Mother Nature. The awesome Japanese Alps, home to some of the world's best hiking and most jaw-dropping views, are an outdoor lover's playground. Skiiers and snowboarders have placed the Hokkaido region of Japan top of the bucket list for good reason – the powdery snow here is among the best and most dependable in the world. Kayakers' hearts may melt at the endless expanses of calm navigable waters, remote, isolated, and home to unique wildlife.

The flavors, textures, and traditions of Japanese food announce themselves at every corner. Whether it's at the local *yatai* (street-food stall), tea ceremony, fish market, Michelin-starred restaurant, or hole-in-the-wall ramen joint, umami is just a slurp away.

It's hard to imagine a place more romantic, a seamless fusion of yesterday and tomorrow. Or a place more diverse, a manic blend of urban mayhem, and a seemingly endless stretch of spectacular terrain.

Zao Fox Village, in Miyagi Prefecture, boasts six different species of fox, who are often visible playing together and angling for treats from tourists.

#The North

If it's sparse and remote with stunningly beautiful vistas you're after, then the far north of Japan delivers the goods. There are fewer people here, residing or traveling, but plenty of opportunities to get up close and personal with people, animals, and the way of life in small villages that possess an almost frontier vibe.

Northern Honshu – more commonly known as Tohoku – and the northernmost island of Hokkaido offer travelers a slice of traditional Japan and access to areas of staggering natural beauty, where outdoor activities from canoeing to hiking or skiing can be enjoyed.

The landscape and the views here are without doubt among the best in Japan. There's a Nordic quality to the land and life here: great swathes of fertile land, ancient forests, cold weather, plentiful ocean views but few people. Hokkaido, the center of Japanese agriculture and aquaculture, offers visitors a chance to sample Japanese produce as its freshest and most delicious.

#Sapporo

Sapporo is the capital of the island of Hokkaido and its largest city, with close to two million people calling it home.

The city is best known for its iconic beer, first brewed in the city in 1876 and now exported and enjoyed all over the globe, as well as for its proximity to ski resorts located on the fringes of the city itself or just a day trip away.

This livable city also boasts the annual Sapporo Snow Festival held at Odori Park. In February each year, this enormous park becomes the stage for epic snow and ice sculptures contributed by corporate, amateur, and professional teams.

Swans, the "angels of winter," relax on Lake Kussharo before making the long trek back to their Russian breeding grounds come springtime.

#Lake Kussharo

Three beautiful lakes, Lake Mashu, Lake Kussharo, and Lake Akan, are the hallmark of the Akan National Park in the eastern part of Hokkaido. The park also boasts magical forests inhabited by wild deer (Hokkaido sika deer) and foxes (the Hokkaido red fox), as well as onsen (hot springs) that provide an opportunity for visitors to relax and recuperate.

The strikingly blue and tranquil Lake Kussharo rests in the Kussharo Caldera, the largest caldera in Japan. Sailing, windsurfing, fishing, and other water-based activities are popular here, but it is the canoeing on the ancient Kushiro-gawa River that lures many visitors to the area.

#matingritual

Two red-crowned cranes, which are among the biggest birds in Japan, engage in a mating ritual at a roost site near Otowa Bridge. The Ainu people, indigenous hunter-gatherers in the Hokkaido region, called the birds *sarurunkamui*, meaning "god of the wetland."

#photoopportunity

Each morning scores of photographers, and their expensive equipment, line up on the Otowa Bridge over the often fog-filled Setsuri-gawa River to photograph the red-crowned crane. The cranes inhabit the boundless expanse of wetlands – each pair requires 247 acres as a territory.

#flowerfields

Furano's lavender fields attract hoards of visitors every summer, when the plants are in full bloom. At other times of year rape blossoms, poppies, lupins, lilies, and sunflowers provide a visual spectacle. The best spot to view the flowers is Farm Tomita, with the Tokachi mountain range a spectacular backdrop.

#lavendericecream

Lavender has been cultivated in Hokkaido for over 50 years. With the arrival of cheaper, imported lavender in the 1960's and '70's, the local lavender's function shifted from agricultural product to tourist attraction. Creative minds put it to good use, such as in the manufacture of ice cream, to support tourism.

#cutemountaincottages

The small town of Biei is located at the foot of the Tokachi mountain range in Daisetsuzan National Park (Japan's largest). Among gently rolling hills and vast fields, visitors and locals explore wild woods, go canoeing, or camping. In winter, the town is transformed and is a haven for skiers and snowboarders.

#valleyofhell

When Mount Kuttara erupted 20,000 years ago a huge geothermal crater formed giving rise to Jigoku-dani, or Valley of Hell, with its rust-colored snow-covered mountains. A 5 mile network of boardwalks and trails skirts around hot vents, thermal lakes, hot marshes, geysers, blowholes, and steam caves.

#Snow Sports in Hokkaido

Skiing in Hokkaido – the snow capital of Japan – is on the bucket list of many a powderhound. Weather-wise it is ideally located to draw a reliable deposit of the soft white stuff. Many of the ski areas receive an average of 45 to 60ft annually of particularly dry powdery snow that's perfect for skiing and snowboarding on.

The four outstanding ski resort areas – Niseko, Rusutsu, Furano, and Kiroro – all offer something a bit different. Family-friendly Niseko boasts deep powder snow and four interlinked resorts, while at Rusutsu it's all about cross-country and tree skiing. Furano, in the middle of the island, is loved for its light, powdery snow, and Kiroro offers skiers the chance to get in early, with the action starting here as early as November.

#epic

With 3215ft of vertical runs, around 1482 acres of terrain, and over 50 miles of trails reaching from a height of 4396ft to 7568ft, Shiga Kogen ski area is epic in size. It launched on the global stage in 1998, hosting various events at the 1998 Nagano Winter Olympics.

#gettingaround

Shiga Kogen comprises 19 ski resorts linked via the slopes and a transport system consisting of 52 lifts, gondolas and a shuttle bus. A European vibe exists thanks to the ability to navigate villages on skis or snowboard. Yakebitaiyama, the largest resort, has the best terrain park and snowmobile area in Hokkaido.

#Sendai

Sendai, known as the "city of trees," is also a place of Samurai legend.

The city is synonymous with the great feudal warlord, Date Masamune, and 400 years on he still makes his presence known here, particularly at the Sendai Castle site and his final resting place, Zuihoden mausoleum.

On the main streets of Sendai zelkova trees burst with greenery in summertime and red leaves in fall, while cherry blossoms are in plentiful bloom during spring on the grounds of the Sendai Castle ruins.

The Tanabata Festival, held every summer here, is a riot of paper lanterns, costumes, and decorations.

For the culinary minded, beef tongue is the local delicacy in Sendai – grilled, seared, stewed, or in a soup.

RIGHT A slope car travels through a beautiful tunnel of cherry blossoms in Funaoka Castle Ruin Park.

#warrior

The inspiration for Japanese period dramas, global computer games, and perhaps even Darth Vader's helmet, samurai warrior Date Masamune was a successful warlord of the 16th and 17th centuries. A statue on horseback at Sendai Castle overlooks the city he founded and the stronghold he built.

#kokeshi

A signature of the Sendai region, kokeshi dolls were originally created as children's toys by villagers in the nearby mountains making use of wood from cherry, Japanese maple, and Japanese cypress trees. Each doll is one of a kind, and nowadays they are collectors' items and the focus of festivals and trading fairs.

#Central Japan

Japan's core in terms of geography, culture, and outlook, the central part of the country is the heartbeat of the nation. After all, here is Tokyo.

It's the largest city in the world as ranked by land area, population, and density – there are over 16,000 people per square mile living in the capital. Tokyo is a metaphor for the country at large, a place where Japanese efficiency meets out-there youth culture, where ancient temples are dwarfed by high-tech skyscrapers. There's no better place to experience the fusion of past, present, and future that is Japan.

The jaw-droppingly photogenic Japanese Alps rise sharply in the region's center before spreading north to the dramatic Sea of Japan coast. Here world-class skiing, hiking, and onsen can be enjoyed. Kanazawa and the post towns on the Old Nakasendo Route ooze history and culture: wooden houses, cobbled streets, Shinto temples, and tearooms that served lords and kept geisha are beautifully preserved for visitors to enjoy.

#Gunma Prefecture

Part of the Kanto mountain range, the mountains of Akagi, Haruna, and Myogi provide the centerpiece to Gunma's abundance of natural beauty. Gunma has many mountains across its landlocked mass, but these three are special and revered as Shinto deities.

Heavily forested mountains occupy much of the area, but Gunma also holds the source of the Tone-gawa River, and the greatest basin area of any river in Japan – for which it's known as "Tokyo's Water Tank."

Gunma has more than 200 onsen, including some of the best and most remarkable in the country. These include the number one in Japan's Top 100 Onsen, the first designated Nationally Certified Onsen, and one of the Three Beautifying Onsen in Japan.

RIGHT The Fukiware Falls have been dubbed the Niagra of East Asia and declared a Natural Monument of Japan.

#bestonsen

Kusatsu Onsen has ranked number one of the Top 100 Onsen selected by travel gurus for 14 years in a row. It boasts the most hot spring water discharged – amounting to around 230,000 barrels of hot water daily. The waters originate in the pristine pine and larch forests of Mount Shirane, an active volcano.

#perfecteggs

Onsen tamago (hot spring eggs) is a popular breakfast food in Japan, though maybe not always cooked the traditional way. It seems spa waters have the perfect temperature for soft-cooked eggs, with the added advantage that they could be left unattended for a few hours while cooking.

Located on the Yukawa-gawa River, Ryuzu (meaning Dragon Head) Waterfall is flanked by trees which turn yellow and red during the fall-leaf season, adding to the dragon-like appearance.

#Nikko

Scattered among green, hilly woodlands, Nikko is one of Japan's top attractions. It's World Heritage–listed temples and shrines convey to modern eyes the wealth and power of the Tokugawa shogunate (1603–1868). However, Nikko was founded in the 8th century by the Buddhist priest Shodo. Thus Nikko's main sights are Buddhist temples and Shinto shrines, often housed in the same buildings.

The Nikko Toshogu Shrine is the most famous site in Nikko. This elaborate shrine complex reached full completion in 1636 and is the final resting place of the founder and first shogun of the Tokugawa shogunate, Tokugawa Ieyasu. Decorative wood carvings adorn the gates and exterior walls of countless buildings at the shrine. The two-story Yomeimon Gate, a designated National Treasure, otherwise known as Sunlight Gate, exhibits an astonishing collection of 500 such carvings.

RIGHT Statues of Jizo, the deity who protects dead children and unborn babies in traditional Japanese Buddhist teachings. It is believed that as the babies did not have the chance to build up good karma on earth, Jizo smuggles the children into the afterlife in the sleeves of his robe.

#prettysakebarrels

A wall of colorful sake barrels lines the pathway to Nikko Toshogu Shrine. When displayed near a Shinto shrine, such barrels are called *kazaridaru*, meaning decoration barrels. The custom is to donate sake to the temples and shrines as an offering for the gods.

#worldheritagesite

The Nikko Toshogu Shrine complex consists of 55 buildings set in a moody, misty forest. Established from a single mausoleum, the entity is estimated to have taken 17 months, required the manpower of over 400,000 carpenters, and cost the modern-day equivalent of 40 billion yen to build.

Tokyo from above, with Tokyo Tower in the distance.

#Tokyo

Tokyo is a city of the future and the past. Cutting-edge architecture, neon signs, and high-tech skyscrapers bedazzle the skyline but at ground level cobblestone streets and lantern-lit alleyways lead the way past wooden houses and artisan shops to ancient shrines. Glimpses into the past of this one-time shogun's capital can thus be seen on the streets as well as on the kabuki stage, at a sumo tournament, or under the cherry blossoms.

One of the planet's most densely populated cities, Tokyo somehow manages to have a calm and efficient vibe with public transport running on time, squeaky clean streets, and low crime rates.

Foodies and shopaholics are well served in Tokyo, a city that's been awarded the world's highest volume of Michelin stars, and some of its most affordable, too.

And of course, it's a people-watching paradise, with the kooky and the cool on display in neighborhoods from Shinjuku to Shibuya.

#skytree

At a height of 2080ft, Skytree is the world's highest stand-alone communications tower. Since opening in 2012, it's become an icon of the city. The high-tech tower sits at the center of Tokyo Skytree Town, with its many shops and restaurants, an aquarium, and planetarium.

#don'tlookdown

The second of two observation decks at Skytree, Tembo Gallery's spiral ramp winds up to the highest viewing point at 1476ft. Floor-to-ceiling windows offer panoramic views across the region and a glass floor provides the view downwards. Touch screens orient the visitor at the swipe of a finger.

#imperialpalace

The Imperial Palace occupies the site of the original Edo Castle. In its heyday this was the largest fortress in the world, but little remains today apart from the moat and stone walls. The Imperial Family lives here and you can check out their digs on January 2 and December 23 each year.

#seeingdouble

Tourists and locals often gather at the Nijubashi Bridge, the official entrance to the palace. The beautiful stone bridge's graceful arches span the moat. A second, iron bridge stands behind it, and when viewed at a certain angle they appear to be one, giving rise to the name Nijubashi, "double-level bridge."

#cherryblossom

Hanami (cherry blossom viewing) provides a chance to reflect on the ephemeral nature of life, or a good excuse for an outing with friends, depending on your point of view. What's beyond debate is that Ueno Park, home to over 800 cherry trees, is the place to do it.

#swanpedalo

Shinobazu Pond is a large natural pond located in Ueno Park, one of the many charming green oases in Tokyo. For a view of the park, the cherry blossoms, or just a moment away from the hurly burly visitors can hire a row boat, a pedal boat, or a pedal boat in a the shape of a giant swan. And why not?

#tokyotower

A Japanese icon, Tokyo Tower was based on the design of Paris's Eiffel Tower. At 1090ft tall, it is the world's highest self-supporting iron tower. The Main Observatory and the Special Observatory provide views of the Tokyo Bay Area and, on a clear day, Mount Fuji.

#littlehistory

The quirky Edo-Tokyo Museum vividly recreates Tokyo's past through interactive displays that start with a life-size replica of the Nihonbashi Bridge. Scale models of towns from the Edo, Meiji, and Showa periods are dotted with intricate figurines. Woodblock prints and samurai swords are among 2500 objects on display.

#sumolegend

Mongolian-born Kakuryu Rikisaburo was introduced to sumo wrestling by watching it on TV as a teenager. His determination led to a move to Japan and a rise through the ranks. He has been a member of the top *makuuchi* division since November 2006 and has earned nine special prizes, seven for technique.

#menonly

The Grand Sumo Tournaments are held in odd-numbered months and last for fifteen days. Matches are held daily. Sumo originated in ancient times as a performance to entertain the Shinto deities. Rituals associated with this men-only sport endure to this day, such as symbolic purification of the ring with salt.

#restinpeace

Yasukuni Shrine in central Tokyo commemorates Japan's war dead. Founded in 1869, this Shinto shrine is the resting place for over 2.5 million people enshrined here. Their lives are documented in the form of written records, noting their name, origin, and date and place of death.

#lanternfestival

First held in 1947, the Mitama Matsuri, or Lantern Festival, is an annual event held at Yasukuni Shrine to honor the spirits of the dead. As many as 30,000 paper lanterns light the way to the shrine, and there are also traditional dance and music performances as well as exhibitions held at the festival.

#fishybusiness

The Tsukiji Fish Market is the largest wholesale fish and seafood market in the world, moving about 5 million lb of seafood every day – seven times as much as Paris's Rungis, the world's second-largest wholesale market. In dollar terms, that's about US$28 million worth of fish per day.

#tunaauctions

Registration for the auctions begins at 5am and competition is fierce. During the first auction of 2010, a tuna weighing 511lb was sold for 16.28 million yen (US$175,000). It was bought jointly by one of the city's most upmarket restaurants and a Hong Kong–based chain of sushi bars.

The Kaminarimon (Thunder Gate) at Senso-ji houses a large red-and-black paper lantern. The original lantern burned down in the late Edo period. It was rebuilt in 1960 and is renewed every decade with the current lantern dating from November 2013.

#Senso-ji

According to legend, Senso-ji Temple was created when a statue of Kannon (the Buddhist goddess of mercy) was miraculously pulled out of the nearby Sumida River by two local fishermen in the year AD 628. Senso-ji was built by villagers to house and honor the statue. It later became the epicenter for the development of Edo culture (1603–1868).

Senso-ji is the oldest temple in Tokyo and the religious heart of the city. Many people believe that the Kannon deity enshrined here has the ability to bestow physical benefits on earth. Some 30 million people visit the temple every year, perhaps in search of help from the goddess.

RIGHT The Five-Story Pagoda at Senso-ji is said to contain partial ashes of Buddha. The original was created in 942 but the current structure was rebuilt in 1973. It is a designated National Treasure and the second-highest pagoda in Japan.

#healing

A large incense burner called a *jokoro* sits in front of the main hall of Senso-ji. Sticks of incense are offered. To take in the purifying and healing powers of the incense the hands are cupped and smoke waved toward the head or body part that is causing pain or creating difficulty.

#blessingorcurse

Fortunes written on strips of paper (*omikuji*) are available, traditionally from wooden drawers, for a small offering at Shinto shrines. The paper provides a blessing or curse of different degrees. The custom is to leave the *omikuji* behind if it's not a good fortune, traditionally tied around the branches of a pine tree.

#Shinjuku

Boom, boom, shake the room, it's Shinjuku boys and girls. The beating heart of the city, Shinjuku is the Tokyo of your imaginings: bright and beaming neon lights, mad and madding crowds, tall and taller buildings, hustling, bustling streets, and high energy galore.

Shinjuku equals shopping, feasting, and partying. Packing in several huge department stores, music stores, electronics stores, and hundreds and hundreds of bars and restaurants, the district caters to every imaginable taste.

Shinjuku is divided into Higashi (east) and Nishi (west) by the train lines that run through the station. West Shinjuku exudes wealth and power with its towering skyscrapers, including the Tokyo Metropolitan Government Buildings, or "Tocho," which see the coming and going of 13,000 Tokyo bureaucrats every day. The east side is down at heel by comparison, but here is real life: the lights ("red" and neon), crowds, restaurants, and bars associated with modern Tokyo.

#secretbackstreets

In the backstreets of Shinjuku is a somewhat secret area called Golden Gai where there are over 200 bars, clubs, and eateries crammed into six skinny alleys connected by passageways so narrow only a single person can pass at a time. Each bar only seats about 7 or 8 people.

#nationaltipple

Previously known as "Sake Plaza," the Japan Sake and Shochu Information Center in neighboring Ginza provides a wealth of information and computer-based data all about Japan's national drink, plus there's the *nihonshu*, or tasting area, where you can sample a few varieties and buy a bottle or two to take home.

#spoiledforchoice

Shinjuku is one of the key battlegrounds for ramen in Tokyo. With over 200 ramen outlets here, the choice is overwhelming and it seems every restaurant has a long line of eager beavers waiting for their lunchtime noodle fix. Ramen, originally from China, is now a Japanese fast food.

#foodieparadise

Shinjuku is a foodie's paradise, a place to get on the sushi train, visit an eatery dedicated entirely to tofu, dine in Michelin-starred restaurants (there are around 240 to choose from and 11 of those have three stars, more even than Paris), or pick up a bento box of goodies at the railway station.

#Shibuya

At (perhaps) the most famous intersection in the world, when the lights turn red, they all turn red at the same time in every direction. Traffic stops and pedestrians surge from all sides, marching headfirst into the organized chaos. It's located at the heart of Shibuya, and it's an enduring and iconic image of Tokyo.

Shibuya boasts shopping, nightclubs, bars, and eateries a plenty. More than 100 boutiques showcase the latest in Japanese fashion. Shibuya is the center for youth fashion and culture, and it's the precinct that's launched a thousand fashion and entertainment trends.

The food court at the the Tokyo Department Store next to the station, known as Tokyu Food Show, offers a mind-numbing display of gourmet eats from grilled eel or octopus on a stick to bento boxes, sushi, or hand-crafted Japanese chocolate.

#subway

With 882 stations on 14 lines, Tokyo's subway system is a monster, albeit a tame one. Yamanote Line, one of the busiest, carries 3.5 million passengers daily. People line up at marked spots on the platform and wait quietly for passengers to disembark before boarding. Efficiency and courtesy are Japanese hallmarks.

#sweetdreams

First conceived by Kisho Kurakawa in Osaka in 1979, capsule hotels consist of pod-like rooms (more like compartments) stacked together. Crawl inside, sit up (just), or lie down. Amenities include a light, an air conditioner, an alarm clock, and, maybe, a TV, power outlet and radio. Not for the claustrophobic.

#mostvisited

Built in 1920 to venerate Emperor Meiji (1852–1912), under whose reign Japan opened up to the West, Tokyo's most famous Shinto shrine is wonderfully serene and austere. Surrounded by the huge Yoyogi Park, with 120,000 trees, Meiji Shrine has an almost rural feel, and is the most visited religious site in Japan.

#biggate

The 40ft torii gate at the entrance to Yoyogi Park is made of 1500-year-old cypress. The gate marks the transition from the outside world to the sanctity of Meiji Shrine and it's normal to bow before walking through it. Access is to the left and right as the center aisle is the path of the gods.

#Harajuku

Just a 5-minute train ride from Shinjuku Station, Harajuku is prime real estate for people-watching and destination central for fashion lovers and shoppers.

Harajuku has been the epicenter of Tokyo teen subculture for decades, and it's still nurturing unorthodox, wild, and idiosyncratic styles even as global brands like H&M and American Eagle Outfitters have landed.

The main action station for street fashion, wacky foodstuffs, and quirky personalities is Takeshita Street, while the neighborhood's other main thoroughfare, Omotesando Avenue, presents a more relaxed vibe. Sometimes referred to as Tokyo's Champs-Elysees, this is where you'll find international flagship stores, cafes, and restaurants.

With extreme neon street styles at one end of the spectrum and off-the-runway designs at the other, Harajuku reigns supreme as Japan's forward-thinking fashion capital.

#rockabillyrebel

Every Sunday rockabilly dance crews gather at the Harajuku entrance of Yoyogi Park and perform to 1950's rock 'n' roll music. Young people from different subcultures gather at the park to show off their styles, including Lolita, gothic, deathrock, cosplay, fairy kei, Fruits, or rockabilly.

#sugaroverload

The food on Takeshita Street lives up to the area's wacky image. Rainbow cotton candy, cake pops, and the legendary crepes add a blast of creativity, color, and sugar to the streetscape. Competing crepe stands provide every filling imaginable, from strawberries and cream to chocolate eclair or jelly donut.

Forest of Numbers by Emmanuelle Moureaux at the National Art Center is intended to represent the decade of the future from 2017 to 2026.

#Roppongi

Expensive bars and exclusive restaurants are the signature of this lively entertainment district popular with tourists and locals alike.

During the daytime, the vast Roppongi Hills skyscraper complex draws the crowds eager for a view from its observation deck, or a chance to peruse designer fashion boutiques and the Mori Art Museum, with its rotating exhibitions of international contemporary works. The nearby National Art Center, one of Asia's largest exhibition halls, is a mammoth gallery with a similar focus.

#bigspider

On an elevated plaza at Roppongi Hills stands *Maman* (2002), created by the late French-American artist Louise Bourgeois. The giant spider is situated at the end of a number of walkways that all seem to lead to it. Bourgeois' series of spider sculptures has featured around the world.

#viewsviewsviews

At the center of Roppongi Hills is the 780ft Mori Tower, one of the tallest buildings in Tokyo. Much of the tower is office buildings and home to Japan's IT industry, but the first few floors have restaurants and shops and the top few an observation deck (the city's best perhaps) and modern art museum.

Minato Mirai 21 is a seaside urban area in central Yokohama whose name means "Harbor of the Future."

#Yokohama

Japan's second-largest city with a population of over three million, Yokohama is a short hop of 30 minutes from Tokyo by train, and is the capital of Kanagawa prefecture.

After the isolation of the Edo period, Yokohama was one of the first ports to be opened to foreign trade, cementing its growth from fishing village to major metropolis. But it still retains a relaxed vibe with uncrowded streets (relatively) and a breezy bay area. The pulse of the city may be measured by the creative arts scene, thriving microbreweries, funky jazz clubs, and international dining scene. A Japanese quirk may be found in the range of unusual museums on offer here, including the Cup Noodle Museum and the Ramen Noodle Museum.

「木学」と「気学」で家造り受賜りま

快適な空間を必要とする子育千代

工夫された家が必要な現役時代

ゆったりと終生住み続けたい塾世代

あなたのライフスタイルをじっくりみつめ

豊かで楽しく暮らせる家造りのお手伝いをします

表札から商いの看板承り

もうやめよう　ビニールクロスの家
あなたの家造ります
創美

家具の修理再生〜製作

お店の出店計画〜設計施工

#Kawagoe

An historic castle town near Tokyo, Kawagoe retains the feel of old Japan that so many visitors yearn to experience. Here's the place to do it.

One-time center of power, Kawagoe Castle, can be visited although is largely ruins apart from one significant building that was home to the feudal lord.

But it's the streets that captivate. Kawagoe retains the two-story *kurazukuri* architecture of its old merchant warehouses, as well as numerous temples and shrines. Many of the warehouses are now artisan stores selling traditional crafts and gift stores.

Museums can be found housed in elegant examples of early-20th-century brick, cement, and stone architecture.

Kawagoe cuisine is famous, with its sweet potato, *unagi* (eel), and various outlandish Japanese confectioneries.

#candystreet

Kashiya Yokocho (Candy Street) is a small back alley where a handful of stores sell old-fashioned sweets and snacks. The town is famous for it use of sweet potato: sweet potato chips, sweet potato ice cream, sweet potato coffee, or even sweet potato beer, brewed at the local Koedo Brewery.

#mochi

Customarily eaten on New Year's morning, these sticky sweets, called *mochi*, started life as glutinous rice that was pounded into a thick white paste. The paste is shaped into small balls and flavored and colored in infinite variety.

Sunrise over Lake Kawaguchiko,
overlooked by Mount Fuji.

#Hakone

Offering serene onsen, traditional inns called ryokan, jagged, misty mountain scenery crowned by Mount Fuji, and great hiking opportunities, Hakone is Tokyo's favorite weekend escape and a hot spot for international travelers too.

Mount Fuji, the tallest and most famous volcano in Japan, is at the heart of the action in Hakone. The backdrop to serene Lake Ashi, the fuel for steamy, bubbling Owakudani Valley and the source of heat for its infamous hot springs, Mount Fuji is the muse for hikers and tourists keen for a glimpse of her iconic slopes and summit.

RIGHT **Hikers descend Mount Fuji via the Yoshida Trail.**

#hakoneropeway

The 30-minute journey on the Hakone Ropeway in a carriage with huge windows allows visitors to take in the views: the crystal-clear blue waters of Lake Ashi, the rising volcanic fumes of Owakudani and Mount Fuji on a clear day. A stop mid-way enables exploration of Owakudani.

#ahoythere

From Togendai the Hakone Pirate Ships cruise the length of Lake Ashi providing a stunning ringside view of Mount Fuji. Calm, cool Lake Ashi is nature's looking glass for the mountain. And if it reminds you of a scene from a woodblock print or painting, that's probably because it's been the inspiration for many of them.

#sulphurvalley

Bubbling, steaming Owakudani stinks. Of sulphur, that is. It's hardly surprising, given its location in a volcanic valley. There are a few hiking trails around the Owakudani station, but there is one that you can't miss. The 15-minute uphill trek to the egg-boiling site, where you can sample the goods.

#blackegg

Kuro-tamago (black eggs) are cooked in batches in the bubbling natural pools of Owakudani. Visitors can take the Hakone Ropeway or hike to see the action in person. Sulphur turns the shell black but inside it's a regular boiled egg. Legend says eating one will add seven years to your lifespan.

#onsen

Hakone's hot spring resorts, or onsen, are legendary and there's no better way to relax after a hard day's sightseeing than with a soak in the mineral-rich hot waters known for their healing properties. Bathing in communal baths means being comfortable going naked in the presence of strangers.

#ryokan

For a more private experience, Hakone boasts numerous Japanese-style inns, or ryokan. Visitors can choose a slick, modern resort, or something more traditional, such as the former country home or summer villa of an aristocratic clan or Imperial Family member. Exquisite ambience and pampering is non-negotiable.

#greenfields

Tea cultivation on the slopes of Mount Fiji is thought to have begun as early as the 1200's, and now accounts for 40% of the nation's tea production. Serious tea fans come here the weekend before the Golden Week holidays (in early May) to photograph the new tea leaves.

#nicecuppa

Tea plays a critical part in Japanese culture, and the associated ceremony has more than a thousand years of history. The process is less about drinking tea, and more about ritual. The host of the ceremony considers the guests with every gesture and the goal is to deliver a cup of tea that comes from the heart.

Sunrise at Mount Tsubakuro (9065ft).

#Japanese Alps

Only two hours from Tokyo, the awesome Japanese Alps provide visitors with some of the country's best skiing, hiking, onsen, and Instagrammable photo opportunities.

Also known as the Hida Mountains, the range rises sharply up from near the border of Gifu and Nagano before spilling north to the Sea of Japan coast. All but one (Mount Fuji) of Japan's 30 highest peaks are here.

The popular Tateyama Kurobe Alpine Route, also known as the "Roof of Japan," provides spectacular passage over the mountains. Along the way, the Tateyama Snow Corridor is flanked by massive walls of snow.

Kiso Valley in Nagano, with its well-preserved traditional towns, runs alongside the mountains of the Central Alps.

RIGHT At the top of Mount Tsubakuro is Enzanso, one of the oldest mountain huts in Japan. The five-to-six hour hike there starts with forest giving way to mountaintop granite ridge paths. Helpful pitstops afford amazing views of the Northern Alps, the Azumino River Valley and even Mount Fuji.

#greatwallsofsnow

The Tateyama Kurobe Alpine Route opened to the public in 1971 and is famed for its snow walls, which stretch up to 65ft high. Murodo has the heaviest snowfall in the world. It takes three months to open up the snow walls trail for visitors.

#cheekysnowmonkeys

At the Jigokudani Monkey Park visitors can see Japanese macaques (snow monkeys) bathing in a natural hot spring. The monkeys, who live in large social groups, are accustomed to humans, which allows for up-close observation. Photo opportunies peak in December to March when they are often covered in snow.

Multi-colored carp glide through the pond water at Kenrokuen Garden in Kanazawa.

#Kanazawa

A compact city, pretty and historic Kanazawa coalesces around a green core formed by Kanazawa Castle Park and Kenrokuen Garden. Ranked as one of the top three gardens in Japan, Kenrokuen provides the visitor with a place of tranquility where carp flit through deep green waters, plum and cherry blossoms signal the arrival of springtime, and a traditional teahouse provides a perfect rest stop.

Kenrokuen, which means "having six factors," is so-called because of the six attributes that are considered to create the perfect garden: spaciousness, tranquility, artifice, antiquity, water, and views.

Adjacent to the gardens and in the center of the city is Kanazawa Castle, home of the Maeda family that headed the Kaga clan, one of the richest and most powerful during the Edo period. The Maeda family also had exclusive rights over a gold mine, which accounts for the city's love affair with the precious metal — here you'll find sake flecked with gold flakes, cakes and sweets with gold coating, and the like.

RIGHT **The Uchihashi-tei teahouse and Kasumiga-ike pond, the largest pond in Kenrokuen Garden, in Kanazawa.**

#flyingbullet

The Shinkansen, or bullet train, proved a very important initiative for Kanazawa. When ticket sales opened for the first journey in March 2015, they sold out within 25 seconds. Japan's high-speed bullet trains reach speeds up to 199mph and can zip from Kanazawa to Tokyo is just two and a half hours.

#morethanhospitality

A unique food scene has emerged in Kanazawa centered around the idea of *omotenashi*. Often translated as hospitality, it's a particularly Japanese thing: esthetics and rituals designed to welcome. Eating sushi in Kanazawa is special. There are varieties of fish here that never make it to the capital city.

Traditional wooden townhouses called *machiya* could once be found throughout Japan and have been particularly well preserved in Kanazawa. The city has established an artisanal school called Shokunin Daigaku for young architects wanting to learn how to preserve these traditional wooden houses.

#Kiso Valley

Running along the scenic, forested Kiso Valley, the old Nakasendo road, also known as the Samurai Trail, connected Tokyo (formerly Edo) and Kyoto in the past. In days gone by, members of the Imperial Family were required to travel this route to interact with citizens, while feudal lords and ordinary people also used it. It would have been a difficult task in this area of steep mountain paths, passes, and cliffs.

The 342-mile Nakasendo is dotted with 69 *juku* (post towns, which arose as rest stops), 11 of which are located in the Kiso Valley. The 4.8-mile trail between the post towns of Tsumago and Magome is generally considered to be the most impressive section of the Nakasendo, and walking this route is one of Japan's most rewarding experiences.

Along the Kiso Valley, a few post towns, particularly Magome, Tsumago, and Narai, have been preserved to look as they did when they served travelers of the Nakasendo.

#stepbackintime

The 42nd of 69 post towns on the Nakasendo Road, Tsumago is one of the best preserved in all of Japan. Cars are not allowed on the main street during the day, and phone and power cables are concealed giving the appearance and atmopshere of the Edo period.

#highstreet

The main street of Tsumago offers plenty of choice with souvenir shops and galleries selling wooden carvings, foodstuffs, indigo-dyed clothing, lacquerware, and other locally produced goods, as well as noodle restaurants, Japanese confectionery shops, and historic inns (*hatago*).

#halfway

Narai marked the halfway point between Kyoto and Edo. The largest of the post towns along the route, it was known as Narai of a Thousand Houses (the wooden homes there stretch that far). Winter here is severe. In February, locals light a candle placed in a container made of ice for the Narai Ice Candle Festival.

#helpwiththemenu?

Located on very precipitous terrain, Magome is unusual among the country's post towns. The walk here is steep. The effort is rewarded by the beauty of the town which includes many shops and restuarants in traditional low rise wooden buildings. Japanese language skills are a plus for understanding the menu.

The Nakabashi Bridge in Takayama stretches over the Miyagawa River, linking Sanmachi-Suji with the rest of the city.

#Takayama

A quaint village atmosphere fills the air in beautifully preserved Takayama. It's most famous for the Sanmachi-Suji historic district. The *san machi*, or old streets, exude the charm of yesterday, boasting original historic buildings built from cedar or cypress, often stained black or brown with soot or tannin. The three quaint streets that make up the Sanmachi-Suji district are lined with traditional houses, shops, restaurants, sake breweries, and cafes and are among the most picturesque in Japan. Museums, galleries, and temples are plentiful here too.

A highlight on the calendar is the effervescent Takayama Festival, a biannual event held in spring and fall each year and one of Japan's most beautiful festivals. Intricately crafted festival floats (or *yatai*) parade the city, each one a testament to the region's history and offering the chance to see the apex of hundreds of years' worth of artistry and craftsmanship.

RIGHT Lion dance performers run down the steps during the Takayama Festival parade.

#geta

There's no difference between right and left feet in this traditional footwear, and the subtle toe movements required to keep feet steady on the flat wooden base stimulate acupuncture points, promoting blood circulation. Geta-inspired clogs are developing a bit of street cred outside Japan.

#wagyusushi

Hida beef is a highly esteemed brand of kuroge wagyu beef from the Gifu area in central Japan. Black-haired Japanese cattle are raised to produce beef of the topmost quality, meeting stringent industry standards for marbling, color, texture, and aroma.

Gion is Kyoto's most famous geisha district. It is filled with shops, restaurants, and teahouses where geisha entertain.

#Kyoto

Kyoto is a city soaked in all the magic, mysticism, tradition, and romance of old Japan. It is said to be home to over 1000 Buddhist temples, each offering up a place of serenity and reflection often surrounded by abundant natural beauty.

Amid this backdrop, tourists linger; geisha scurry to rendezvous; merchants sell tofu, tea, or *washi* (Japanese handmade paper) at stores on old market streets; and locals buy produce at bustling markets, tuck into bowls of ramen for lunch and attend kabuki theater performances in the evening.

Rituals and traditions are critical here and Mother Nature dictates many of them. No Kyotoite would dare write a letter without making a reference to the season. The city's geisha change their hair ornaments monthly to celebrate the natural world. And Kyoto's confectioners create sweets that reflect whatever is in bloom that season.

RIGHT **Kinkaku-ji (the Golden Pavilion), covered in glittering gold leaf, shimmers in the light over its neigboring pond. Both the temple and the Zen garden surrounding it are iconic Kyoto travel experiences.**

#famousicecream

If you're going to eat green tea ice cream anywhere in the world, it ought to be Kyoto. This sweet delicacy has become synonymous with the city, which claims to be its home. Shinpachi Chaya's famous Ganzo green tea soft ice cream is said to have been the first green tea soft serve ice cream sold in Japan.

#geisha

Though geisha can be found throughout Japan, Kyoto is considered the birthplace of geisha culture. Seeing a geisha in a quiet traditional street like this one (Sannen-zaka leading up to Yasaka Pagoda) is a special moment. Geisha are professional artists of Japanese traditional culture and entertainment.

#visitanytime

A designated World Heritage Site and National Treasure of Japan, the Daigo-ji, founded in AD 874, is one of the world's most beautiful temples. It's a sight for all seasons. Vivid greens beckon in spring and summertime, while red maple leaves erupt in fall and wintertime brings a white dusting of snow.

#lookandlisten

The Sagano Bamboo Forest provides one of Japan's most iconic images: a grove of gently swaying trees reaching up to the sun-speckled canopy above. It's a visual spectacle enhanced by sound. The Ministry of Environment added the bamboo's rustling and stirring soundtrack to its official 100 Soundscapes of Japan.

#weirdandwonderful

Centuries-old Nishiki Market caters to locals, who do their shopping here, and tourists, who soak up the hustle and bustle, listen to the unintelligable cries of traders, smell the fresh fish, pickled vegetables, roasted chestnuts and ground sesame, and gape at the weird and wonderful produce on offer.

#eatifyoudare

The food stalls at Nishiki Market provide the opportunity to try all manner of Japanese delicacies, including *takotomago*, baby octopuses stuffed with quail eggs, which the market is famous for. Deep-fried chocolate balls, ice cream, soybean tea, pickled vegetables, and tuna sashimi are other options.

#wisemonkeys

The small temple of Yasaka Koshin-do is dedicated to Koshin-san, a guardian warrior, and the three wise monkeys. In the Koshin faith, the Koshin-san helps those who strive to better themselves. The hut containing his likeness is hung with *kukurizaru* – colored balls of fabric.

#iwish

The balls at Yasaka Koshin-do represent control over desire-driven behavior. Visitors place one of their desires into a *kukurizaru* and leave it with Koshin-san. Desires are thought to stop wishes coming true, therefore Koshin-san takes away the desire and thus grants the wish.

Trails lead into the forest of the sacred
Mount Inari. The hike to the summit is
a two-to-three hour round-trip. Along
the way, there are multiple small shrines
with foxes, food and wine offerings, and
miniature torii gates.

#Fushimi Inari Shrine

For over 1300 years, Japanese people have gathered at the Shinto shrine complex of Fushimi to pray for prosperity, safety, good health, and the fulfillment of wishes. It is now one of the most iconic sights in all of Japan for visitors.

The entire 765ft-high mountain of Inariyama, on which the Fushimi Inari Shrine is located, is considered a precinct of the shrine. Smaller shrines, sites containing the remains of deities, worshipping stones engraved with deities' names, and shrine gateways (known as torii) are scattered across the mountain.

Cheap souvenirs are everywhere, but for the big bucks it's possible to donate a gate (prices start at 400,000 yen for a small one) which will then be inscribed with the donor's name. Individuals can donate, but more often national and local businesses take up the offer.

RIGHT **A torii gate at Fushimi: torii represent the entrance to a sacred shrine in the Shinto religion.**

#headoffice

Dedicated to the god of rice and sake by the Hata clan in the 8th century, Fushimi Inari is a complex of shrines and shrine gates spread across an entire mountain in Southeast Kyoto. This shrine is head office for some 40,000 Inari shrines located throughout Japan.

#thousandsofgates

The seemingly unending path of vibrant vermillion gates winding through the hills behind Fushimi Inari Shrine is an iconic image, providing motivation for many travelers to visit Japan. It is known as Senbon Torii ("thousands of torii gates") for good reason – it's thought that some 32,000 gates and sub-gates line the path.

#foxeseverywhere

The fox is thought to be the messenger of the god of rice, Inari, and is a persistent theme at Fushimi Inari Shrine. The keys often depicted in the mouths of the foxes are keys to granaries. A fox with more than one tail is wiser and more powerful. A red scarf around a fox's neck is meant to ward off ill spirits.

#foxyema

Ema are prayer plaques found at nearly every shrine in Japan. For a small fee, visitors can write their hopes, dreams, wishes, or prayers on them and leave them hanging at the appropriate spot. At Fushimi Inari Shrine, the fox motif is used, with each *ema* cut into the shape of the wily creature.

The famed semi-wild deer at Nara-koen park in Nara.

#Nara

The picturesque city of Nara was Japan's first permanent capital and contains eight World Heritage Sites, rivaling Kyoto as a repository of Japan's cultural legacy.

The centerpiece is the Daibutsu (Great Buddha) housed at Todai-ji Temple. The big guy is up there with Mount Fuji and Kyoto's Golden Pavilion (Kinkaku-ji) as the most-visited attractions in the country.

The soaring temple Todai-ji presides over Nara-koen park, a beautiful expanse of greenery filled with fascinating sights and famously tame sika deer. Once considered sacred messengers of the Shinto gods, and thus protected, they were later hunted to near extinction although the population is safe today.

Nara is a compact city that can serve as a handy day trip from Kyoto.

#gettingaround

The rickshaw is thought to have been invented in Japan in the 1860's. Pulled rickshaws created employment for male laborers within Asian cities in the 19th century. The word rickshaw originates from the Japanese word *jinrikisha*, which literally means human-powered vehicle.

#bigbuddha

The Daibutsu statue weighs in at a whopping 551 tons and stretches a towering 49ft tall, with a 17.5 ft-long face and hair crafted from 966 individual bronze balls. Creating this massive bronze Buddha occupied much of Japan's bronze production during the 8th century when it was made.

Osaka Castle strikes a pose in a modern urban cityscape of high-rises. An expansive lawn-covered park and complex network of moats, turrets, and walls surrounds the impressive central tower.

#Osaka

Tourism is on the up and up in Japan's third-largest city. Traditionally considered a transit hub en route to Kyoto, in 2016 it experienced 9.4 million tourists arriving to explore the city in its own right, an increase of 31 percent on the previous year.

A lovely river cuts a meandering swathe through this otherwise bustling metropolis, which isn't pretty in a traditional Japanese sense. It's concrete clothed in neon and a hodge-podge of architectural styles. What it lacks in charm and looks, it makes up for in pace, energy, and letting the good times roll.

This city is all about fun. Fun for some means food and nightlife, and Osaka boasts plenty of that. The unofficial slogan of the city is *kuidaore* ("eat till you drop"). Famous Osaka treats include *kushi-katsu* (deep fried skewers of meat and veg), *takoyaki* (octopus balls), and the savory cabbage pancake (*okonomiyaki*).

RIGHT The flashy Dotonbori district lines the south bank of the Dotonbori Canal and is a great place for relaxing, dining, and kicking back.

#facelift

Osaka Castle, built originally in 1583–85, was largely destroyed in the wars of the 17th century. The current tower was completed in 1931 and completely renovated in 1997, with fresh white walls, new roof, and gold leaf decoration. Eight floors inside are dedicated to exhibits on the castle's history.

#daytrip

Built around 1886, Takimichi is a walking trail which leads to the famed Minoh Waterfall. The trail snakes alongside the stream, with Japanese cedar, cypress, maple, and cherry trees on both sides of the trail providing a stunning and changing visual spectacle throughout the year.

#busybusy

Busy, bustling and always open for business (some restaurants here never close), Dotonbori is a popular shopping, entertainment, and foodie destination. At night the blazing heart of Osaka is illuminated in neon lights and mechanized signs, including the famous Glico Running Man and Kani Doraku crab signs.

#hustlebustle

Osaka's Kuromon Ichiba Market, established in the early 1900's, contains over 150 shops situated along a length of 1902ft and is thought to attract over 25,000 visitors daily. A source of cookware, it's dubbed "Osaka's Kitchen" by locals. Seafood – raw or cooked – is a speciality to buy or eat here.

#streetfood

Dotonbori is packed with delicious eateries, including the classic sushi trains and ramen booths. The street food is plentiful and splendid here too. Two Japanese classics that have been widely exported to the West, *takoyaki* and *okonomiyaki*, originated in Osaka, so this is the place to try them.

#comfortfood

The ultimate in Japanese comfort food, these crispy little balls called *takoyaki* are stuffed with all kinds of deliciousness such as minced octopus, scraps of tempura, green onions, and pickled ginger. Served in a box with a variety of toppings, they can be taken on picnics, snacked on, or eaten at home on the couch.

Also called Shirasagijo (White Heron Castle) due to its white outer walls, Himeji Castle serves as a classic example of early 17th-century Japanese architecture.

#Himeji

Himeji is famous for the magnificent Himeji Castle, considered to be Japan's most beautiful and best preserved feudal castle. The castle is designated both a National Treasure and a Unesco World Heritage Site. Its construction in wood combines function with esthetic appeal.

The castle comprises 83 buildings and sophisticated defense systems such as impossible-to-scale walls and narrow windows for ejecting missiles or boiling water onto enemies.

The origins of the castle date to 1333 when a fort was constructed here and occupied until 1871. At that time many castles were destroyed to mark the end of the feudal period but Himeji survived in a new role as military barracks. It has also endured proposed development, an unexploded bomb, and an earthquake, so chances are it's here to stay.

Visitors can see a couple of sculptures
near the harbor before they even get
off of the ferry at the "art Island"
of Naoshima. Yayoi Kusama's yellow
pumpkin perches at the end of an old
concrete pier.

#Naoshima

Some 30 years ago, Benesse Holdings, a global publishing and educational conglomerate, bought a big hunk of land on the small island of Naoshima's south side. They needed a place to store former organizational head Soichiro Fukutake's collection of contemporary art, which included pieces by the likes of Andy Warhol and Claude Monet.

Benesse hired world-renowned architect Tadao Ando, and over two decades he designed museums and luxury accommodation on the island. The buildings follow the contours of the landscape. One museum is almost completely underground, with open courtyards and skylights bringing in natural light.

Fast forward to today and some 800,000 tourists flock to the island's art festival each year. The resident population of 3000 people has declined from 8000 in the 1960's. Many empty homes were purchased by Benesse and gifted to artists to create so-called "art houses," a nifty idea for putting empty spaces to good use by creating galleries within them.

#The South

The further south you go, the milder the climate in Japan, giving rise to a very different vibe than in the central and northern areas.

The island of Okinawa is anchored in the East China Sea about midway between Japan and Taiwan. It's said that the people here live especially long lives. And visitors may be tempted to stay forever, as the combination of laid-back people, emerald seas, white sands, and a tropical climate is mesmerizing.

Further north on the island of Kyushu, the steaming spa town of Beppu welcomes visitors to rest and recuperate at one of many onsen. Beppu sits on the flanks of Tsurumi volcano. The island as a whole has more active volcanoes than any other Japanese island.

Further north still, the city of Hiroshima is a special place of pilgrimage for many visitors to Japan. In addition to the bomb-related sites, Hiroshima contains the incredible Itsukushima Shrine, which seems to float on the sea.

The great torii gate – boundary between the human and spirit worlds – at Miyajima, Hiroshima.

#Hiroshima

By 1876 the current borders of the city of Hiroshima had been established, following several centuries of argy-bargy among the regional warlords, which began in 1589 when Mori Terumoto gave Hiroshima its name and built a castle in what is now Hiroshima City.

The city was instantly and comprehensively destroyed by the dropping of the atom bomb in 1945, and the story since has been one of recovery, rebuilding, and renewal thanks to the efforts of its citizens.

Hiroshima today displays many touching tributes to peace that include the Peace Bell, Children's Peace Monument, Flame of Peace, Cenotaph for Atomic Bomb Victims, Hiroshima Peace Memorial Museum, and Hiroshima National Peace Memorial Hall.

Just north of the Hiroshima Peace Memorial Museum is a small crop of phoenix trees that survived the bombing. Saplings grown from seeds taken from the trees have been distributed across the globe as part of Hiroshima City's activities to promote peace. Green shoots continue to appear on the trees every spring providing an enduring symbol of endurance.

#enduringsymbol

At 8:15am on August 6, 1945, the first atomic bomb was dropped on Hiroshima. The Genbaku Dome was located directly underneath the explosion, but it somehow avoided destruction and the remains still stand today. The people of Hiroshima decided to keep this tragic reminder of war intact.

#shrineinthesea

Built originally in the 12th century, Itsukushima Shrine is among the most striking in Japan. A bold and unique structure that protrudes proudly from the sea, the colors of the shrine contrast with the blue water and green backdrop making for a vision that's not easily forgotten.

Women relax in a hot sand bath at a Beppu resort.

#Beppu

One of Japan's most famous hot-spring resorts, Beppu, produces more hot-spring water than any other in the country. Beppu is home to almost 3000 hot springs, making it the second-largest source of thermal spring water in the world after Yellowstone National Park in the United States.

The Hells of Beppu are spectacular hot-spring sites created for viewing rather than bathing, and each one has been converted into its own miniature theme park. A popular tourist activity in the area is to visit all eight hells.

Takegawara Onsen was the first onsen in Beppu. This beautiful building was built more than a century ago, in the Meiji era. Today, almost every hotel and ryokan in the city provides access to hot springs as a service to customers. There are an unrivaled range of baths to be enjoyed here, including standard hot water baths, mud baths, sand baths, and steam baths.

RIGHT **Steam rises from the ground at any given opportunity in the city of Beppu.**

#seahell

The largest and most beautiful of the "hells," Umi Jigoku (sea hell), features a pool of cobalt blue boiling water (208°F), which stands at 656ft deep. In the spacious gardens, manicured lawns are framed by red torii gates and cherry blossom trees.

#relaxandunwind

During Golden Week – when most Japanese take their holidays – some 60,000 visitors stay at Beppu's onsen resorts. The healing waters of the mineral-rich onsen provide the perfect environment to relax and unwind.

There are approximately 150 *yatai* (street-side food stalls) spread out across the city of Fukuoka, but most can be found in and around the Tenjin and Nakasu districts.

#Fukuoka

Japan's sixth-largest city is comprised of two former towns, the Fukuoka castle town on the west bank of the river and Hakata on the east. The two towns merged in 1889 under the name Fukuoka, though the name Hakata is still used.

Fukuoka's proximity to the Asian mainland has attracted a rich, cosmopolitan population. And it's a city that seems to be constantly on the move, with modern buildings, booming shopping malls and even direct flights from Europe. This regeneration hasn't happened at the expense of the old town, with the result that in a small space there are ancient temples rubbing up against high-tech gadgetry or artisan craftspeople.

A warm and friendly city, Fukuoka is a pleasing place to pass time – eating, shopping, visiting, and exploring.

RIGHT Built in 1995, the Reclining Buddha at Nanzoin Temple is enormous: 135ft long, 36ft high and weighing in at 330 tons – about the weight of a jumbo jet.

#yatai

Yatai is the name given to street-side food stalls in Fukuoka. Stalls a few feet long produce delicious food each evening before packing up and disappearing only to reappear the next evening. While ramen is a *yatai* speciality, each stall offers different dishes reflecting regional cuisine.

#holyramenbatman

It's soup and noodles elevated to a religion. Noodle shape and thickness and toppings vary depending on dish, location, or shop. But it's the soup base that defines ramen. There's salt-based *shio* ramen, soy-sauce-based *shoyu* ramen, miso ramen, and *tonkotsu* (pork bone) ramen.

The beautiful Takachiho Gorge with the Gokase River running through was created by volcanic flow from Mount Aso.

#Miyazaki

Nature plays its part in the appeal of Miyazaki. With one of the warmest climates on the main islands of Japan, resorts, beaches, and sports facilities erupted here and provided the foundation for Miyazaki to become a top honeymoon and domestic-travel destination during the second half of the 20th century.

While this has since waned, interest in visiting the extensive natural parks and long coastline of Miyazaki remains. Takachiho to the north and Kirishima to the southwest are both places to enjoy the beauty of nature.

At Takachiho, there are two perspectives from which to experience the gorge – from below or above. The water is calm and easy to navigate by rental boat, allowing an up-close view of the cliffs of volcanic basalt and 55ft Minainotaki waterfall. A paved path runs along the top of the gorge providing stunning views all along the way and at some points on the trail you can look straight down to the river below. The trail eventually leads to the Takachiho Shrine.

RIGHT **Stunning yellow leaves shine above the boaters in Takachiho Gorge.**

Turquoise lagoons, pristine beaches and fun times at Okinawa.

#Okinawa

Okinawa is the largest of the Ryukyu Islands, a semi-circular archipelago of over 150 islands stretching between southern Japan and Taiwan.

The surrounding emerald seas are among the world's most beautiful, boasting coral reefs, abundant marine wildlife, and white-sand beaches. Not surprisingly, snorkeling and scuba diving are top of the to-do list here, where the climate and environment are subtropical.

It's Japan, but not as we know it. Once the Ryukyu Kingdom, Okinawa has a unique culture and history that differs from the mainland in terms of language, cultural traditions, and food. Okinawa is relaxed, less intense, and less ambitious than the rest of Japan. While Japan looked inwards, Okinawa looked outwards.

Okinawans are said to have the longest lifespan of any people on earth – men can expect to live to about 84, women closer to 90.

First Published in 2018 by Herron Book Distributors Pty Ltd
14 Manton St
Morningside
QLD 4170
www.herronbooks.com

Custom book production by Captain Honey Pty Ltd
12 Station Street
Bangalow
NSW 2479
www.captainhoney.com.au

This edition first published in 2019.

Text copyright © Captain Honey Pty Ltd 2018

The moral right of the author has been asserted.

All rights reserved. No part of this book may be reproduced or transmitted by any persons or entity, including internet search engines or retailers, in any form or by any means, electronic or mechanical, including photocopying (except under the statutory exceptions provisions of the Australian Copyright Act 1968), recording, scanning or by any information storage and retrieval systems without the prior written permission of the author.

Cataloguing-in-Publication. A catalogue record for this book is available from the National Library of Australia

ISBN 978-0-947163-64-8

Printed and bound in China by Shenzhen Jinhao Color Printing Co., Ltd

1 2 3 4 5 6 7 8 9 10

PHOTO CREDITS

Front cover: thipjang
Back cover: Juri Pozzi

Images used under license from Shutterstock.com
except for pages: 1, 2, 6, 77, 78, 81, 93, 131, 179, 196 © Unsplash
90, 102 © istock